THE CROWS WERE LAUGHING
IN THEIR TREES

Other Books by Peter Conners

Of Whiskey & Winter (poetry)
Emily Ate the Wind (novella)
PP/FF: An Anthology (editor)
*Growing Up Dead: The Hallucinated Confessions of a Teenage
    Deadhead* (memoir)
*White Hand Society: The Psychedelic Partnership of Timothy Leary &
    Allen Ginsberg* (non-fiction)

THE CROWS WERE LAUGHING
IN THEIR TREES

PETER CONNERS

WHITE PINE PRESS / BUFFALO, NEW YORK

White Pine Press
P.O. Box 236
Buffalo, New York 14201
www.whitepine.org

Publication of this book was made possible, in part, with
public funds from the New York State Council on the Arts,
a State Agency.

State of the Arts

NYSCA

ACKNOWLEDGMENTS

Many thanks to the editors of the following publications where these poems first
appeared, sometimes in a slightly different form:

"Animals and Other People" appeared in *Fiction International*; "The Coffee Barista's
Experiment" appeared in *Fiction International* and *City Newspaper*; "Bite the
Pomegranate" appeared in *Diagram*; "Meat Zoo" appeared in the online version of
Verse; "Waiting" and "Entrance: Where We Leave From" appeared in *elimae*; "One
Morning at the Lab" appeared in *Paragraph*; "The Owners of Things" appeared in
Unpleasant Event Schedule; *Charred Remains* appeared in *The Bitter Oleander*; "The
Lonesome Orphan" appeared in *AfterImage: A Journal of Media Arts & Criticism*;
"Balloons & Boys" appeared in *New Madrid*; "Along the Ribbon," "The Directions
That We Move (slight refrain)," "Old Man in the City" appeared in *Redactions: Poetry
& Poetics*; "Tragic Old Love" appeared in *Tacenda*; "Tragic Old Love" and "And So It
Is" appeared in *While in the World* (Foothills Publishing, 2003); "Discussions with
the Bridesmaid" appeared in *Hotel Amerika*; "Long House" appeared in *Sentence*; "One
Night a Girl in the Suburbs," "Monkey Spider Bites," "The Church & The Steeple"
appeared in *Flights*; "The Directions That We Move" appeared in *Greatcoat*; "One
Night a Girl in the Suburbs" appeared in *The Slush Pile*; "Postcard from the Banquet,"
"Four Little Girls," "Into the Sky Falls an Executive" appeared in *Pinstripe Fedora*; "To
Have Done with It" and "The Church & The Steeple" appeared in *Double Shiny*.

Cover design: Steve Smock
First Edition.
ISBN: 978-1-935210-20-7
Printed and bound in the United States of America.
Library of Congress Control Number: 2010933051

Table of Contents

We leap awake and what we see
fells us   .

Let terror twist the world!

—William Carlos Williams
Paterson, Book Two

I

Bite the Pomegranate

The juice of a red pomegranate seed impregnated by the memory
of its mother branch in the family grave. My pledge to you is
exactly equal to the sum of these parts: one trembling uvula, the
pomegranate seed of the mouth, three frozen fingers, the last
heartbeat of the modern prophet, blue mercury, vinegar tincture,
a tire blowing, withering, as it kills a porcupine on a Southwestern
freeway. The majority of mothers are not human. Blessed is the girl
who observes brains in the bloody pustules set before her. Blessed
the incisors popping those pustules devouring the places where
memory bleeds toward violence against one's self. Heal thy self.
Love the shadowy movement of thine own imagination. Eat your
fruit. Fall from trees.

II

Animals and Other People

❖

The monkeys are difficult to evict. My Uncle Lester is a monkey. If I were a monkey he would be a monkey's uncle but not necessarily a monkey himself. But that is not the case. He is a monkey. And the monkeys are difficult to evict.

❖ ❖

My cousin Terri is a panda. Soft, big-bellied, stuffed full of leaves and stems of leaves. If you punch her breadbasket she giggles and burbles like corduroy laughing between thighs.

❖ ❖ ❖

All of my friends are warthogs. Neither fish nor fowl, that long drip off the saber's tooth is saliva, not blood. Add salt around the rim of this spectacle. Mix with menthol. My friends are warthogs with foam rubber tusks. It tickles me when they fall down drunk.

❖ ❖ ❖ ❖

Mashed fish and buttered squash in tiny jars. Feathers slick with mucus and sweat: my infant is a penguin. Arms tight to his sides, swaddled and helpless, he will only fly when he steps away from crevasses and the ledges of sandboxes. In this, too, he is a penguin.

❖ ❖ ❖ ❖ ❖

When I play with hummingbirds it is easy to break their hollow bones. Their yellow blood decorates the inside of pickle jars. In the morning, they sing me down to breakfast. We forget our dreams. In the morning it is easy to forget your dreams.

❖ ❖ ❖ ❖ ❖ ❖

Hummingbird my father bays at the moon. He keeps me awake.

One Night a Girl in the Suburbs

There is a door behind the door that conceals everything she does not want to learn. Father delivers the woman's enemy to her doorstep while Mother makes a list of betrayals while Sister's mind is populated by the ghosts of wallflowers: fall leaves swirl around the noose the girl has tied to the tree shadowing the grave of the family dog. Doll feet swinging in the yard. Her mind is made up. *One day* was so elusive it became unspeakable. Their foundation slopes East forcing cracks into spidery basement letters the family uses to interpret the neighborhood. This is a tiny script. Irony makes atrocity palatable to Brother and to the friends of Brother who fill the house with their mild ejaculations. The girl stands in the driveway imagining the limbs of her family tumbling fist over elbow into the ocean.

The Lonesome Orphan

✦

The knotty twine of tension extracted through a hole in my right molar—the Princess climbed up through my sinuses, the cavities giving up the secrets I had tried so long to brush away, melt away, but the vine grew stronger with each deliberate act of neglect until the hole, alone, was left to be filled with white.

✦ ✦

They scraped the razorblade sidelong over the thin tissue of skull shaving layers of flaked skin into a pile then brought the razorblade down over and over until the white scales made serpentine lines: absorbed through the eyeballs of the captain's most loyal men.

✦ ✦ ✦

Inside the miniature temple was an enamel statue carved out of the left incisor of the court jester into the shape of the Queen's late lover, the captain of the guards. The temple itself was located in the heart of the Queen which was displayed for prisoners on Tuesday and Sunday evenings inside the gilded bell jar out of their reach.

✦ ✦ ✦ ✦

The Orphan placed each tooth beneath the stuffed sackcloth upon which she rested her head but when she awoke there was never a piece of brass or a pulpy fig encrusted with sugary juices—instead the teeth sat side-by-side until they formed a bed upon which the orphan lived and died.

The Boy had learned to suck his thumb while the Orphan was waiting.

The Orphan and the Boy never met.

Monkey Spider Bites

The spider monkeys of tiny rebellion keep their guns cocked and their wars even closer. It is no surprise then that we find ourselves making love to the spider monkeys. *Perhaps you are my father.* One cold day in June the spider monkeys coiled their limbs and they died. *Perhaps you are the father.* In the mist of the forest the spider monkeys swing off silent ears of mourning. Milk nourishes the mosquitoes through veins of baby spider monkey eyes; the mother disapproves of all the monkey achieves, thus denying the pleasure of the monkey. The caged monkey eats disease. He nominates himself monkey among monkeys: the eye shadow is slutty, the results inconclusive, monkeys scale brick walls and hang from intertwined vines spitting venom through incisor syringes (milky venom, banana peppers). The chief spider monitors the welfare of the doe-eyed fauna, the mewl of dandelions, the wallowing of willows whilst his boy lover licks his palm and begs for mercy.

Postcard from the Banquet

Mr. Cooper had yet to explore the far corner of his tangled property. *Have you ever been stung by a dead bee?* It was the spot where a window cleaner killed himself before Mr. Cooper moved into the house. *There is no sunshine in Kafka's head.* Not Mr. Cooper's window cleaner, mind you, but the man dangling from the Dogwood nonetheless streaked Mr. Cooper's mind. *He dreamed us today—the sky was too dark for anything resembling wakefulness.* Aware that the metaphorical properties of Death were exhausted, the visiting scholar vowed to avoid it altogether. *Endings are difficult; tattoo that on the back of your eyelids.* Mr. Cooper commissioned a song absolving the lonely of mortal sins. As always, the accompanist arrived too late.

The Coffee Barista's Experiment

❖

In the twentieth hour the spider plant waved at Shelly. It was in that instant that you glimpse the outside world before the bathroom door latches shut. As she eased down her zipper the image blazed:

❖ ❖

In the twenty-seventh hour Shelly imagined the city built of sugar cubes. While she mixed chocolate syrup into the fourteenth mocha of her marathon shift, she pictured the bank, the pet store, the police station, video store, the entire city made of sugar cubes. If it rains, she thought, we will all taste sweet freedom.

❖ ❖ ❖

The roosters were not a surprise. Already, dolphins had ordered raspberry scones. An enormous cockroach munched coffee grounds until its belly distended, pulled taut and round. The roosters were too loud though. Their talons scratched and clicked, beaks cutting through biscotti with an unsettling snap. They ordered round after round of black coffee, eyeing Shelly with suspicion that turned bitter, increasingly ominous. It had been forty-seven hours of work, no sleep, and countless cups of coffee passed across the wooden countertop.

❖ ❖ ❖ ❖

The roosters slurped their coffee: Shelly put hands over her ears, hummed to herself, turned up the music to shut out the noise.

It was almost dawn. She couldn't bear to think of what might happen next.

Tragic Old Love

The man is waiting for sex imaging a world where coyotes slip under stream rollers to become paper thin accordions. The woman has a son now and a black eye and a husband in Europe and everything is fine. *I think of you every time I'm broke*, she says, days after their world broke. And he thinks, *Now?* Eight days ago he penned into his notebook: The most subversive act in our society is to just be still. He made notes for a skewering piece on authors writing novels for the purpose of product endorsements: appropriate when plague was metaphor. Now he gets nervous when he doesn't feel worried; finds himself staring at her infant in a baby seat by the bed wondering what a one month old dreams about. Her future: he jolts himself back into America whenever he drifts away. Three days ago no planes flew overhead, no one threw peace or gang signs, television was for information. Now he awaits a lover who grew into a stranger to deliver him from the tyranny of this infant future. Four days ago music held the place for his most important memories; now she lowers herself down knowing that she will be back in Europe before the rubble is cleared. Time has a new beginning. And he will be alone.

One Morning at the Lab

They put the mouse into a cage and told him he wasn't a mouse. They loved him because he was a mouse. But he couldn't be a mouse anymore. He could be a white mouse with black tips on his ears and moist pink nostrils: not a mouse. He could not be an elk. He was in love at the time, but no one asked him whether that was the case because it was non-cage related. He was not a mouse was all. That was all: he wasn't a mouse. He was given the name Lucky Star to make him feel more celestial but the next day it was changed to Sun and then Vapor and then God and finally Mickey which gave them all a good laugh. When he sang it was as if memory itself was sighing and shivering with delight. This was the best part of their day.

Waiting

❖

Having the picnic would feel like dying twice. Once when your heart stopped. Once when the party ended. So Lisa did not want the picnic in the first place.

❖ ❖

The picnic was held at Sour Ridge Pavilion: Greek salad with bow-tie pasta, deviled eggs, a keg of light beer beneath the eaves of a rented pavilion. Hamburgers, hot dogs, and Italian sausage lined the park's grill meat-to-meat soaking up noxious licks of briquette flame. Her husband worked the grill while teenagers tossed a Frisbee.

❖ ❖ ❖

It was the summer the cicadas crawled out after 17 years underground. They screeched mated and died. Insect bodies lay in black mats across the East Coast. Tymbals, translucent wings, coarse sensitive hairs knotted together. They were shoveled, crunched. They smelled of landfill and rotted earth.

❖ ❖ ❖ ❖

There is an old black man with a cane and trucker hat seated in the window of an art gallery. I pass him every morning on my way to work. He looks like an art installation. And then everything looks like art installations. Even sunlight and random sounds on the street feel piped in and phony; arranged for a positive review.

❖ ❖ ❖ ❖ ❖

As the procession of cars followed her hearse between the iron gates and down the narrow path to the open grave I waited for someone to appear with a tray of hors d'oeuvres and Chardonnay. I kept waiting for the artist to show his face.

Meat Zoo

The monkeys had been burning all morning. In the midst of it all, peanuts were sold at a discount. Polar bears batted seal corpses across their habitat. The cows were made of ground beef with two lamb eyeballs wedged into their heads at odd angles. Penguin skins were doormats; orange duck feet propped open lavatory doors. The crows were laughing in their trees.

The Owners of Things

❖

The man's wristwatch outlived the man by decades. It had wonderful adventures; took up with a bi-coastal drug dealer who relished it for sentimental reasons unrelated to the previous wearer.

❖ ❖

Porcupine quills bedecked with beadwork. The boy batted the earrings around the kitchen floor like a dog worrying a clean, white deer skull. Or a porcupine. The boy batted the earrings around the kitchen floor like a coyote worrying a porcupine.

❖ ❖ ❖

The CDs sang their songs to each other. If only she would he might dance the way he did to those head-banging reminders of bonfires and thrill rides. The man moved to Slayer the way toddlers dance to any music: disjointed, utterly absorbed, the definition of tragic.

III

Movements Forward, Movements Away

It seemed like enough to give without giving too much. This ivory comb. This pewter cup. This blue speckled egg. This leather pouch filled with marbles. This quilt sewn from the memories of generations, the baby blankets of ghosts, the longings of raindrops merging into ponds where the boy and the girl swam down holding hands. The legend says that they never returned. But this is not quite true. The boy and the girl walked the streets in the cold hours just before dawn, they made vows into the old man's ear, they placed secrets into the old woman's ear, they brushed their fingers through the teacher's auburn hair, they left traces of pond silt in the eyes of sleeping children, the footsteps of the boy and girl meandered through every alley, every bedroom, they held hands as they had done so many years ago and swam through the town as they swam through the pond, under their lives, outside the eyes of the people who would relinquish them to cautionary tales meant to shame poor children into being fearful adults. But the boy and the girl would never know such fear and shame. They could never imagine.

They were looking for water. Most did it with sticks branched into Y shapes quivering when over underground basins, but not in the girl's family. The girl used the boy as the women in her family had always used the men: *Take my hand*, she instructed him, *not too tight, only enough to feel the pressure.* The girl's long dress brushed over the scrub picking up a thin layer of dust that puffed out invisible clouds as they moved together. She made a small joke about the moisture in his palm. Her eyes were closed to the high color of his cheeks. They made it as far as the pasture's edge when the sky tore an unholy purple above them and thunder and lightning bore down together—no chance to count beats or run for the barn, only more water, more water, as if the bottom of a bucket had been blown out. *Stop*, the girl said, her eyes still closed, fingers resting gently in the boy's open palm. *We are almost there.*

❖ ❖ ❖

They fell in love in the most common of ways. The girl's hair hung long and brown down the back of her blue dress; just long enough to reach the edge of bad Milo's desk where an inkwell was mounted, brimming. A meniscus of temptation. The boy heard the knocking of the girl's stiff soles down the empty school corridor; her head flashing past children reciting numb multiplication tables and state capitals Moments before, the boy closed his eyes and saw the girl's chin yanked up and back as Milo pulled her hair down and submerged the tip of her ponytail deep into his well. The boy saw this happen before the girl's face registered her shock; before she dashed out of the classroom as the ponytail wrote letters of humiliation in black ink across the back of her blue dress. The boy saw Milo leave school that day and set off down the wooded path behind the chapel that led to his uncle's house. The boy saw Milo confronted on the path. The boy saw Milo defiant, trembling, posed in hackneyed boxer's stance, no one else around; Milo's head snapping as he absorbed punch after punch. The bloody, instant bruising. Milo, weary and beaten, kicking stones along the way home to his uncle who would beat him again for tearing his good school pants and getting whipped by another kid. The boy would give the girl the courting gift of the pain of another boy, a tormentor boy, a tormented boy, this bad boy, their unity.

❖ ❖ ❖ ❖

A boy promised a girl a fireworks display for her birthday. But he had no fireworks and no means to buy them. The boy thought of all the things his grandfather had taught him, but none would surprise the girl because the girl knew all the tricks and together they lived in a world of their own imagination. But somehow fireworks must razzamatazz in the sky—kapow! The boy must make a magic the girl had never seen and could never predict. This would not be easy. The girl knew so much. But the boy had learned one more thing that he had never tried, one more ministration that might save them both. The boy came to the girl's window on the night of her birthday and whipped it with branches until the girl emerged and made her way down to earth. Their steps were lit by the yellow balloon overhead and the bright stars they had visited and made vows upon since they were children. And somewhere the old man, somewhere the old man. The boy took the girl to the top of Windsong Hill and instructed her to lay down on her back—she giggled, nervous, but did as instructed. The boy stood over the girl—a boy-man silhouette against the enormous moon and everywhere stars. *Are you ready?* the boy asked. The girl nodded and closed her eyes, waiting. *No,* the boy said, *keep them open.* The Milky Way was thick and bright overhead and each and every light shining down knew their names and the promise they would bring. The boy raised his hands to his sides and swiftly clapped them together over his head. As he did, the entire sky—stars, moons, galaxies, solar systems—went dark. The sky was pure black. The boy pulled the only light in the universe from his pocket and placed it on the girl's ring finger.

IV

And So It Is

In the beginning God was created without form and face upon the Deep upon the face of the waters the firmament Heaven were under the firmament from waters which were above the firmament and so it was that God called the Earth dry land and divided Light from Darkness and gathering together Waters after Beast of his kind cattle Creepeth creeping multiplied filling the Seas evening and morning were the fifth day green Herb dominion every living thing bearing seed for Meat every fowl meat and seasons for signs Days for years upon the earth lesser light rules Stars be fruitful be multiplied be Man in our image subdue the Earth and so it was: Genesis.

Long House

I was a slave in another life pine boxes were filled with my body trenches crudely dug too many others piled over my worn trousers flames melted the buckles of my shoes in another life I gathered my children close to shield them from collectors there was nothing I could do please in a moment dear god in another life we fled from mastodons bent on discovering a new means of propulsion smelled radioactivity when the salt gave way to megatons in another life we sat together (didn't we?) in another world the sun was eclipsed by a pack of stars and rabid silence devoured the veldt in another life the musket scorched my eyebrows in another time a brook trickled near my window with trout thick enough to submerge in white flour in another life we powdered dirt on our tongues mashed between our lips and stopped moving in another life rivers made shale into thumbprints visible from mountain peaks in another life the hem of my dress fluttered while the concrete stayed waiting in another life the berries tasted mortally bitter in another life our marriage propelled us beyond what our bodies would allow and we got down on our knees when it was time to be whipped.

Entrance: Where We Leave From

She was tricked by her son who promised her a lollipop at the end of that death tunnel.

The little girl lifted her tramp dress for the man who put his finger inside and wiggled.

Here is the spot where the son leaves his mother, poor womb, demented and alone.

Once upon a time her husband, his father, made love to the waitress there.

The parade goes swimmingly. And then there is pudding.

Here Are Some Things

Do you notice the footsteps on the stairs when no one is walking how they used to make shoes but now they make silence do you notice that sometimes the juice ain't worth the squeeze do you notice that guy with one tooth in his head trying to figure out whether he likes men or women or to play it safe with meth or death or so he says over and along the sidewalk you notice that scar on my forehead by the golf club by the surgery by the one on my spirit longing do you notice the meandering willow tickling the wind and pray it will last in your memory when you expire or when you remember that you're still alive so keep doing what you're doing wake up to yawn in the midst of a manifesto or to bark in the shower or to cower in the face of a tricycle assault and hunker down over a plate of humility wishing it were the pie you ordered wishing your hunger away so much it breaks your insides you want it to last you want it to linger you want it to stay this way but it won't it never does you just touch these memories you try to sing but no one wants your memory alone.

The Directions That We Move

Deer Run East is bereft of haunts this morning. Indians burned the shack to mulch but winter is the Mother: when it is too cold to bury, loved ones must turn to the basement. Affix the spigot, tap the tree (beneath the table tap three table taps). Indian skin the tenor of sun-tough sap; there is no telling how many intentional breaks were heard before temperatures snapped the core of wood to carbon.

My sons dislodged three turkeys in a gulley besotted with tires and iron oxide. It is the fourth turkey that makes you wonder—plump as they will be. To the South there is a dry creek bed; to the North a surviving footbridge. To the South empty bottles; to the North the needlepoint of sun strands affixed to memory. To the North the land from which we issue forth; to the North the mother who bore these small boys; to the North that which we amble toward.

I admit that I regard the raptor at the mouth of Deer Run East as sentry. I fear I admit too much. It is my foot that you will hear in this field, as the seasons move you will find me here before or after sunlight warms the carnage in the woods. Bless these potentialities that move me beyond my own sweat; if I have the power to bless them, then bless them.

My sons see only sticks that they will hit into other sticks. The pollution of this place, the prejudice, the ecology of the fingerling bellies of long-haulers shimmering too close to the bed where water once met the wood buckets of settlers will not touch their games.

I want so badly to tell them ghost stories. Yet they would believe as I believe and this believing together is more than I am willing to call down.

My wife, their mother, awaits our arrival from behind the window.

The Directions That We Move (slight refrain)

History says streets run black with ink
as our feeble words wash away.
But what we really mean is: how can we close
this hole in the sky? The crow darts
through the opening followed by the turkey,
the heron, the Onondaga who hunted this land, the hawk
who surveyed it, the migratory geese who attack
when threatened—well they should, plump as they may be.
I called down the spirits in Nederland and now
I can't send them away. If I told you that a hole opened
in the floor when I spoke "bless them, then bless them"
would you read it as metaphor? My sons believe that I conjure
Indian spirits, so does the drunk slumped
against me on the couch of my friend's house;
it is logical to him, thus I will never fully leave
my old life behind. The root of belief is trust (faith):
salesmen believe little. Most addicts have nothing left.
My being is besotted. These footfalls have wrung me winded,
unbound and singing. I want so badly for you to believe me,
the spirits, the hole in the floor, the hole in the sky,
the sentient beings that hover over my infant's cradle,
the wings I am not allowed to pursue just yet. But your belief,
your trust, your faith is more than ink alone can secure.

Four Little Girls

Four little girls dressed like Catholic schoolgirls for real were walking down a street that cars used for moving their people from place to place when one of the girls stepped out into the street not meant for her stepping while a string of cars like beads on a rosary slowed at the insistence of each one in front of it with the one in very front braking hard kissing front fender bowing close to asphalt when the little girl the other girls called Elizabeth was oblivious but old enough to know better old enough after all for permission to walk this road with friends so that the driver in the front car felt impelled to scold her yell for making him shake and nearly striking her in the road on a day when no little girl in any outfit should be flattened down by speeding vehicles least of all this little girl in this little outfit on this day by they who had no intention of killing anyone no little girl no no little girl no little girl we learn lessons but some just never do.

Balloons & Boys

I understand the impulse to celebrate bits of the boy in the balloons but the balloons are not the boy and the boy is not bits in the balloons. *Some are whispering. Hands are touching.* One day before I heard about the balloons traveling one hundred miles to land on the 14th hole of a golf course I spotted a skinny scared doe scampering down a dense city street with blood in its mouth. *We have not yet arrived at the section of disbelief.*

The man was a junkie with a necktie for his day in court. *Were there balloons mystifying overhead?* He pleaded for the police officers to believe his story: a skinny scared doe had scampered down a dense city street with blood in its mouth. *Some are whispering. Elbows are nudging.*

There was an opportunity here for a bystander to free the man of his doubt and paranoia. The police officers were getting to him. *Have I moved this body before?* There was an opportunity for a bystander to combine the idea of bits of boy being projected into balloons mystifying one hundred miles into a city where a scared skinny doe scampered through midday traffic. There was an opportunity for us all to stand in doubt.

To Have Done with It

Now hear this the ball will drop our souls will explode and we will mime our body ravaged by malady now hear this whereby God is the dissected organ of human retardation now hear this voice penetrates violently not malevolently interstices worrisome in their permeability now hear the fingers of the deaf man gather and stack in blessed memory of the piano stool now hear klieg lights depress the spirit of the actor all the better to inspire the audience to calamity now hear the ball will drop our souls will explode and we will mime our body ravaged and abnormal now hear the creation of volcanoes where none existed now hear this I fell in love with Abyssinia as it sank beneath the feet of Ras now hear this so primordial you must have loved it before swallowing now hear this carnivore who has not yet had lunch now write and tell me when I will be carried aboard the ship now hear this stomach consume itself this reflex now hear carnivore not cannibal said the cannibal now isn't my premise delicious now there are roasted toes and the parts newborns shed toward childhood now you know the ones now aren't I now isn't it now it could not be more so if they were traded for guns for opium for pipes for the tiny shrouds of Musca Domestica this Grunt this Squeal this.

The Church & The Steeple

this is the way we watch humans parade we fold our
hands like this lock step this is the way we know
how we feel we know how we feel like this lock step
this is the way we peel back the fabric our tongues
find their nerve ends like this lock step this is the
way we close our eyes the empty skies fill up like
this lock step into the earth we watch the parades
parade through the earth like this lock step this is
the buzzing of stinger to star our prayers are old
prayers like this lock step a bayonet scar a shrapnel
bazaar the wind through our shelter

The Prayers of Strangers

How could I not have realized that you pray for me? I have spent
weeks waiting for you to sleep. These are the variations on humanity;
the exiles return. When you glimpse the mother standing over
the small girl do you imagine a protective or punitive scenario?
The factors: time of day, proximity to the road, experience of the
viewer, amount of food in the belly. Three relative strangers (they
are both) with good intentions—all—sipped coffee and discussed
monsters. Children love these three strangers, some of them, and
are universally attracted to monsters. In the distance, you glimpse
another scenario: satellite clusters with faces arrayed toward space
and a winged statue overlooking a small, dark city. Do you imagine
this statue to be a Roman god or a fairytale creature—must we read
so much into these things? When I learned that you pray for me I
heard you say "it's very real" and metaphor collapsed. I confess, I
do not pray for you: it makes one so humble to imagine you on your
knees for me. I want so badly to eat your monsters, my stranger, to
make them mine. But we are trapped in these thoughts—mother
standing over daughter—while I long to be praying with you.

Along the Ribbon

"The liner sequencing, the regularity of signs, the clear patterns of ordering, they tell me this is writing, but we don't know what it says."
—Dr. Stephen D. Houston, Anthropologist

Of the Olmecs of Veracruz who etched 28 distinct signs, some repeated, 62 times into a Mexican stone while simultaneously evolving into extinction along the ribbon between 1200 and 400 B.C. the language of Hugo Chavez who smelled sulfur at the U.N. podium while exalting Noam Chomsky thus turning the U.S. Terror Alert to Orange along the ribbon between this body language of the teenage girl at the airline desk extending one pointed toe, another pointed toe, then exhaling into slack existence while mother extends the mother-hand of sighs to the man at the counter whose navy blue vest will never give up its secrets to archeologists in the form of soft serpentine stone 14 inches long 8 inches wide 5 inches thick whispering of insects and lizards in repeating patterns sunk into the concave surface of the rock of the Mesoamerican Poets of the Zapotec of the Maya in Veracruz in Tabasco in my backyard in the expiring of August in the incantations of the black and yellow Argiope spiders winding their letters into language my sons would like me to translate when all my lips will speak all my tools will write is that there is a fire that howls at the center of the earth and we are ciphers on a stone slab awaiting the eye of the youth with the magnifying glass.

Old Man in the City

The boy was a man who was different in the city in which he lived
the city where the boy had learned to cross his hands behind his
back and walk slowly down the middle of noonday sidewalk traffic
without interrupting the flow of humanity that broke around the
rock of him the boy who was a stone who would read the passing
people as they moved by and diagnose the ills he found inside but
never learned to cure them and so he moved through the city waiting
for the one to emerge who could teach him the lessons he hadn't
time to learn who would erase the loss the dislocation the empty
the alone and only when he realized that he was no different than
the oceans that burst around him than the woman selling sweet
potatoes than the man misting oranges than the man and woman
passing unknown on the noonday street who could produce the
messiah if only they stopped to speak only then was he ready for the
one to show himself and only then would he recognize the one and
for years he went like this for years he went like this when he came
upon the window of the shop in the city street with the poster in the
window of rows and rows of alfalfa and one small bare foot holding
fast in the top corner and when he drew back from the window he
saw the reflection in the glass of an old man with a brown straw hat
upon his head in the middle of a city and when he tipped his hat to
the old man the old man tipped his hat in return and together they
went to buy a ticket to someplace new.

Pictures of Ourselves

On our first date we will stare at photographs of each other mumbling words of encouragement for victories everyone has forgotten on our second date we will try to remember our former lives and coming up with nothing we will imagine elaborate scenarios that somehow never involve scraping dung off slaughtered goatskins on our third date we will admit we have never lived before and if we did it was not together and if together it was not in blessed peace until our fourth date when we realize these were not photographs of ourselves after all but photographs of our children dressed in our leather shoes and clothes so comically oversized we had simply mistaken ourselves for shrunken nonagenarians when in fact we were not even our own children which is to say not even ourselves so we decided that after more dates we would have the children in the photograph and ascribe to them all the aspirations we had imagined for ourselves but never achieved on any of these dates in history when you were not Josephine and I was not Napoleon nor Elise nor Bonaparte nor any of these figures we wonder why we must have been something we imagine we study the photographs with our eyes while our knees move against each other in a way that lays the groundwork for some future.

Charred Remains

This is a love letter to the throat of the flame swallower. But this is not intentional, only how I am made. There are memories and there is memory: the fire swallower's knowledge of Homo Erectus's mastery over stones and twisting vines will not help him swallow, nor quench his thirst for hearth or mastication. The horse drawn wagon of the flame swallower rattles away into the violet spotted countryside.

This is a love letter to the wrist of the aerialist. Here is your worst experience. You may have it scrubbed from your memory, but first you must parade it for the entire world. To be wandering in the chatoyant bedroom of eyes. To forget each book the minute it is finished. When you told me you understood me I knew why you were lying: the potion seeps out through every organ you once held dear. Always remember, we are counting on you to make it out alive.

This is the diary of the girl who sweeps the cages. She has fallen through the webbing to emerge inside the lynx's folded paws. The salt and dung of petits champignons on knuckles she enjoys licking: she is a sensualist filling her water pistol with holy wine to shoot spots into the sun. My lover has been gone for many lonely nights. How many times must we cry out your name?

Into the Sky Falls an Executive

A bottleneck of human flesh tussling took them to the edge
where history is dependent on proper amounts of oxygen where
the accumulated loss of thousands of imperceptible connections
pressed her back where illuminated strands flowed through the
wreckage where the traders did not have what they needed where
what they needed existed in water molecules infants clutched
in their fists with night   terrors three days out of the
hospital where chemical properties should not   occur to
them where lick waves on the distance where outside the palace
gravity matters   in ways gravity does not matter and this
is known as physics   and the bloodbath of recent memory
where a man with a letter   opener stabbed into his neck runs
into the copier and falls down dead where birthday's melting
          chocolate where if only a bumblebee where if only a warbler
where market research laughs in glowing red tickets where there is
no hint of the woman who once used chalk and black boards where
milk curdles where a man plucks out his eyes when he notices he
is going blind where every day a woman considers the terms of her
final internment but comes to no conclusions

V

Discussions with the Bridesmaid

❖

I apologize for my hunger: it was not meant to offend.

If by die you mean invisible and ineffectual, then yes. I am conducting electricity like never before.

The leprous leaves of September leap earthward.

❖ ❖

Once gripped by the searing sadness of fall, the world's saddest picnic plays out over the concrete loading docks of a factory.

I want to protect my son, but we are both astounded by the power of garbage trucks.

I got lost on my way to work two times last week; the only days I was scheduled.

❖ ❖ ❖

A father is an obligation heavy with calendars.

So lays the bread and meat of our milk and blood.

The echo inside our desire: the whisper we least admit.

❖ ❖ ❖ ❖

The loop pulls the bow pulls the string pulls the loop pulls the hand pulls the string pulls the sheaths pulls the tendons pulls the bow.

Ephphatha which is "to be open."

My coffin will be equipped with the trappings of success. I will entreat you, my beloved, to hide there.

❖ ❖ ❖ ❖ ❖

Qian which is "in front of, or before."

A bend in the creek hides the basin of rainwater where the Sparrow touches her beak to reflection.

If you will still my hands from shaking. If you will only still my hands from shaking.

❖ ❖ ❖ ❖ ❖ ❖

There is only mourning here only the essence of saffron amid simmering Rose petals.

Why must we always deprive our senses?

Nunchi which is for serendipity beyond awareness.

❖ ❖ ❖ ❖ ❖ ❖ ❖

There is no October here only dead water striders awash in chlorine seas.

> The drift of the skin of November calves.

The echo of the revolution; the magic tips of sulfur.

❖❖❖❖❖❖❖❖

A spider in the corner of the curio cabinet. Beyond the threats the seeds that stain.

> There is no ancient ruin here only melody ancient melody ancient.

> *Mimesis* which is what we say when we've nothing left.

❖❖❖❖❖❖❖❖❖

The wine enters the air beyond the shape of the chalice.

> *And what of betrayal that has no root in prayer?*

You may hold your only child but you must hold the sorrow of this memory alone.

❖❖❖❖❖❖❖❖❖❖

Albedo, the inner lining of the soul, which is the lowest fruit of our days.

> *The walls have eyes. The eyes have eyes.*

The wind shows the sun and the tree the frailty of exposed bone. If by broken you mean earthbound,

> *I apologize for my hunger: it was not meant to offend.*

Notes

"To Have Done with It" in honor of Antonin Artaud's "To Have Done with the Judgment of God." Commissioned in 1947 by Ferdinand Pouey, director of dramatic and literary broadcasts, for French Radio broadcast on February 2, 1948. The broadcast was halted by Vladimir Porche, director of French Radio, at the last minute, roughly one month before Artaud's death. Also from "To Have Done with It" the words "write and tell me when I will be carried aboard the ship" were Arthur Rimbaud's last words.

The epigraph by Dr. Stephen D. Houston in "Along the Ribbon" was taken from the *New York Times* article "Writing May Be Oldest in Western Hemisphere" by John Noble Wilford, published 9/15/2006.

Slightly different versions of "Movements Forward, Movements Away" and "Old Man in the City" were originally written as part of a collaborative poem with Nin Andrews entitled "Fireflies." Thank you, Nin, for the inspiration, and for the term "boy-man" in "Movements Forward, Movements Away."

This book is dedicated to my family—blood and extended—especially Whitman, Max, Kane, and Karen.

About the Author

Peter Conners lives in Rochester, NY with his wife and three children. His books include *Of Whiskey & Winter*, *Emily Ate the Wind*, *Growing Up Dead: The Hallucinated Confessions of a Teenage Deadhead*, and *White Hand Society: The Psychedelic Partnership of Timothy Leary & Allen Ginsberg*. He is Publisher of the not-for-profit literary press BOA Editions, Ltd.

His web site is: www.peterconners.com.

The Crows Were Laughing in Their Trees is set in Bernhard Modern,
a font designed by Lucian Bernhard (1883–1972)
for American Type Founders in 1937.
It is characterized by its small lowercase
with tall ascenders and short descenders.

❖

White Pine Press and the author
thank the following individuals
for their generous support
in the publication of this collection:

June C. Baker
Gwen & Gary Conners
Jan & Gregory Conners
Heather & Steven Ralph
Todd Weiner & Family
Nan & Dan Westervelt